60

INSIGHTS

for Mastering Business Development

By William B. Scheessele

Kathleen G. Scheessele and Nicholas J. Coppings

While the publisher and the author have used their best efforts in preparing this book, they make no representations or warranties with respect to the accuracy or completeness of the contents of this book and specifically disclaim any implied warranties of merchantability or fitness for a particular purpose. The advice and strategies contained herein may not be suitable for your situation. Neither the publisher nor the author shall be liable for any loss of profit or any other commercial damages, including but not limited to special, incidental, consequential, or other damages.

60 Insights for Mastering Business Development
First Edition | March 2012
ISBN-13: 978-1105575082
ISBN-10: 110557508X

Published by Mastering Business Development, Inc. (MBDⁱ)
7422 Carmel Executive Park Drive, Suite 202
Charlotte, NC 28226
(704) 553-0000, (800) 553-7944 | FAX (704) 553-0001
Internet: http://www.mbdi.com

Printed in the United States.

International rights and foreign translations available only through negotiation with Mastering Business Development, Inc. (MBDⁱ)

Dedicated to Nic and Melissa with the help of Becky and Joanne for undertaking and accomplishing this project. We have had the pleasure of working with many exceptional people that have shared with us their words of wisdom. We pass them on to the four of you to understand, live and share with others. Without the vision and initiative of Nic and Melissa this project would never have been undertaken. Without the work of the four of you it would never have been shared with others.

Bill and Kathy

Dedicated to Madeline, Penelope and Elizabeth who make my world turn, my parents and family for always supporting me, my mentors and clients who challenge me to grow each day and to Pete Huntley who instilled in me a love of writing.

Nic

Table of Contents

Chapter 3: Business Development Role Insights

Chapter 4: Self-Worth Insights

Chapter 5: Risking and Resisting Change Insights

Chapter 6: Thinking Insights

Chapter 7: Business Development Relationship Insights

Chapter 8: Business Development Process Insights

Chapter 9: Client Engagement Insights

Chapter 10: Client Engagement Skill Insights

Additional Resources

Preface

Why was this book written?

This book was written to provide insights that challenge the way you think about and approach Business Development and sales. It has been said that there is nothing new in sales, and this book adds little new to the vast quantities of sales and Business Development knowledge that is now available. However, what this book will do is challenge you in the way you apply that knowledge.

Currently, the world economy is experiencing challenges that have not been witnessed in close to eighty years. The need for a new way of thinking to approach the role of Business Development is quite apparent. It is our hope that the insights presented in this book will challenge you to take a different approach to Business Development and to the way you engage clients.

In a challenging economy, proactive professionals who know Business Development have no immediate concerns. Their competition, reacting to the changes in the marketplace are huddling and wondering what to do. The truth is, in a tough economy, about eighty percent of the business that was ever available still exists. Those individuals who know professional Business Development continue to succeed, independent of the marketplace, the product, the company or other external forces. They don't externalize control over their situation, wrongly convincing themselves that external factors make the difference between their success and failure. Instead, they internalize control. They realize the truth in the old saying, "If it's to be, it's up to me."

They embrace responsibility for the position they are in, realizing it is the result of what they have chosen to do or not to do in the past. They have helped create the circumstances they are in, and they take responsibility for working in it. If they see an economic slowdown on the horizon, they begin immediately to transition from reactive to proactive Business Development. They realize there is always enough business in the economy for a progressive Business Development team to win and be successful. It's just a matter of knowing how to go after business proactively.

Remember, you cannot change your actions (behaviors) if you don't change your thinking. Focus on your thinking, and your actions will change.

What is an insight?

The Oxford dictionary defines an insight as "the capacity to gain an accurate and deep understanding of someone or something."

Many of the insights contained in this book began as "Bill's Bullets". These bullets have been used for decades as reminders and prompts as part of our education and professional development programs. The exact origins of some of the insights are unknown, since they have been passed down through the family. Others have evolved over thirty years. Many of these insights apply to your life roles outside of the Business Development realm. However, within this book, we offer them in the Business Development context.

While Bill Scheessele has been primarily responsible for establishing the one liner, it has been left to the rest of the MBD[i] team to expand upon each and provide the substance for the insights.

MBD[i] still publishes at least one new insight every month. There are still many one liners that have not yet been spun into an expanded insight format. If you would like to have access to our monthly insights, be sure to sign up for the newsletter on our website at www.mbdi.com.

What's covered in this book?

The chapters in this book are aligned with specific areas of Business Development, with the exception of Chapter One.

Chapter One contains the insights that are more comprehensive and cover material that could have been included in multiple chapters.

Chapter Two relates to personal and professional Goal Setting and Planning and the insights that deal with this aspect of professional Business Development. Without goals and plans, you will struggle to be successful as a Business Development Professional.

Chapter Three covers the insights that relate to the challenges of the Business Development role. One of the most critical factors for success in professional Business Development is the ability to separate ourselves from our roles, or in other words, the ability to distinguish who we are from what we do.

Chapter Four relates to the insights that address an individual's self-worth and how they see themselves in the Business Development role. Highly successful Business Development Professionals understand the value they bring to the client and understand that the Business Development role does not impact their self-worth.

The insights covered in Chapter Five relate to an individual's ability to "risk" within a role and also address an individual's resistance to change. This is an area where many of us struggle. Change is never easy. There are some people who embrace it, while others resist it at all cost. Business Development Professionals understand how to risk failure and are not afraid of role failure.

Chapter Six covers the insights that tie to the thinking and understanding of psychology required for successful Business Development. Thinking and conceptual limitations are key areas where many Business Development Professionals fail.

The insights presented in Chapter Seven cover the rules and principles of the Business Development relationship. These insights address the relationship between the prospect or client and the Business Development Professional.

Chapter Eight presents Business Development process insights. These insights relate to the individual's or organizations' Business Development process. Building, understanding and using a Business Development process is critical. If you are not following your own process then you can be certain you are part of someone else's process.

The insights presented in Chapter Nine pertain to the Client Engagement Process. Ultimately Business Development is all about

Client Engagement and your ability to gain trust, confidence and information. These insights address how a Business Development Professional approaches and engages with clients and prospects.

Chapter Ten presents insights that address the intelligence gathering skills required to successfully execute the Client Engagement Process.

The Additional Resources section at the end of this book provides information about MBD^i followed by a glossary of terms, and an alphabetic listing of all the insights presented.

About MBD^i

Mastering Business Development, Inc. (MBD^i) is a leading Business Development consulting and professional development firm whose comprehensive Business Development services are utilized by thousands of organizations worldwide. Founded in 1979, MBD^i has provided Business Development resources in the following markets: government services contractors, nuclear, power, energy and utility, biotechnology and pharmaceutical, consulting engineering services and economic development. MBD^i provides solutions to organizational revenue growth challenges by:

- Conducting present state Business Development assessments and formulating recommendations;
- Building, integrating or turning around Business Development organizations;
- Developing and implementing strategic, operational and tactical Business Development plans;

- Evaluating and sourcing Business Development leaders and personnel;
- Designing and implementing Business Development and business acquisition processes that guarantee revenue growth;
- Designing, building and delivering standard, customized or tailored Business Development curricula.

If readers want to contact us to offer feedback on these insights or delve deeper into any of them, please contact us at Mastering Business Development, Inc., 7422 Carmel Executive Park Drive, Suite 202, Charlotte, NC, 28226. (Phone 704-553-0000 or email info@mbdi.com).

Acknowledgements

We extend sincere thanks to the following individuals without whose assistance this book would not have been possible. We appreciate all those previous MBD[i] staff members who have helped with the creation and editing of these insights. A special thanks is in order to Melissa Harper, Becky Donaldson and Joanne Reda. Without your administrative, layout and editing skills, this book would not have finally come to fruition. And, to our good client, Chris Lawrence, thanks for giving us the motivation to finally compile this book

The Authors

William B. Scheessele is Chairman and CEO of MBD^i, a management consulting and training firm located in Charlotte, NC, specializing in Business Development Consulting, Training and Personnel Services.

Bill is a successful entrepreneur, business owner, nationally known speaker/author and highly acclaimed consultant and educator. In all these endeavors his focus is on assisting individuals, companies, organizations and industry groups in learning the fundamentals of professional Business Development. Bill's background is multifaceted. He holds a BS degree from Purdue University's Krannert School of Management and an MBA from Xavier University. After completing undergraduate work in industrial management, he learned the importance of teamwork, leadership and rigorous training as an Army basic combat instructor. Upon leaving the military, he transferred his knowledge and skills into a highly successful sales career, attaining sales and management positions at Texaco and leading international sales for a subsidiary of the Trane Corporation.

In 1979, Bill left the corporate arena and launched MBD^i. Over the past three decades, his firm has become the go to Business Development consulting company for many prestigious government services, energy, engineering, scientific, and technical organizations, both nationally and internationally.

Bill keeps a full speaking and writing schedule and is a National Speakers Association, Certified Speaking Professional (CSP). He is the author of *Winning Conversations, Mastering the Art of Business Development* and serves as a columnist for *Washington Technology*. His articles on Business Development topics have appeared in *Electric Light and Power, Power Engineering, Managing Power, Military and Aerospace Electronics' Defense Executive Newsletter* and *PE* (Professional Engineer) *Magazine*.

Kathleen G. Scheessele is Executive Vice President of MBD^i, a Philadelphia native, she earned a BS in Mathematics and Chemistry from Purdue University and an MBA from Duke University's Fuqua School of Business.

Kathy's career has evolved through many facets over four decades, from scientific research, to STEM education, to Business Development and marketing. In 1979, Kathy joined Bill Scheessele in establishing and growing their firm, MBD^i. Since its inception, Kathy has served MBD^i in many capacities, with the most significant being her current responsibility for the firm's Strategic Marketing.

Kathy has served as President of the Purdue Club of Charlotte, as a member of Fuqua's Alumni Council and is currently active on the board of the Duke Club of Charlotte. Kathy also served on Purdue's College of Science Alumni Council and continues to support Purdue's Women in Science Program (WISP), providing mentoring and assistance to women pursuing undergraduate and advanced degrees at Purdue's College of Science. Professionally, Kathy is a member of the American Nuclear Society (ANS) and Women in Defense (WID).

Nicholas J. Coppings is Senior Vice President and General Manager of MBD[i]. Nic spent his formative years in Pietermaritzburg, South Africa where he attended the prestigious Maritzburg College High School. He completed his Bachelor of Social Science at the University of Natal and holds an MBA from Edinburgh Business School Heriot-Watt University, Scotland.

Nic has over two decades of experience in business management, Business Development and management consulting. His career spans three continents and a wide variety of functional roles. With MBD[i] he has built the consulting practice and has been instrumental in adding to MBD[i]'s client list many of the top 25 US defense contractors, other government services organizations and utility and commercial organizations. He has assisted these companies in the assessment, planning and turnaround of domestic and international Business Development organizations. He has developed, refined and implemented strategic, operational and tactical plans, tailored and customized Business Development processes, assisted in the recruiting and assessment of Business Development personnel and developed and written training programs to implement Business Development processes.

Nic is a successful entrepreneur, having started, grown and sold an IT services company and has an abundance of both retail and merchant banking experience, firstly with Absa Bank, South Africa, then Republic National Bank of New York (HSBC) in London, UK, and Frankfurt, Germany. Early in his career, Nic held a variety of roles with KLF Productions, an event management company, with clients that included Reebok, Mercedes Benz, Coca-Cola, Adidas, Budweiser, SAB-Millers and managed Nelson Mandela's birthday celebrations.

1

CHAPTER ONE:

Comprehensive Insights

The following six insights cover a variety of content areas and could not be contained in any of the other chapters of this book, making these all-encompassing insights.

#1

What Is Business Development?

For more than three decades, we've been challenged to describe what Business Development is all about. More often than not, it's been defined by explaining what it isn't. It's not the same thing as selling. This is a simplistic, inaccurate answer and does a disservice to both perspectives.

Business Development is the process of helping a prospect or client determine their needs or wants from their perspective and secure a solution—whether or not they purchase it from you. It's based on a philosophy and methodology that builds a long-term, trust-based relationship. On the other hand, selling is a largely transactional process that is usually defined in vendor or provider terminology for products and services. Both perspectives are needed and valuable in the marketplace.

While the concept of Business Development can be used effectively in all industries, it's an exceptionally appropriate fit for leveraging knowledge or intellectual capital to solve problems. Over the span of more than thirty years in consulting, we've challenged our engineering, energy, biotech/pharma, utility and government services clients to do just that—use what they know about people, business, money and technology to initiate a dialog and build relationships as trusted advisors. What binds these diverse industry groups together is their valued expertise, which is leveraged into revenue and profit.

By no means are we expecting engineering, science or IT professionals to become salespeople. However, individuals can learn to transcend from the colleague to the partner role. Professionals learn that understanding people and what motivates them to buy is more vital to the Business Development process than their technical knowledge. This evolves through embracing Business Development thinking, expertise and behaviors to strategically meet client needs and, as a consequence, produce revenue for their firms.

In Business Development, revenue generation is never an accident.

#2
What Is Your Business Development Culture?

Every organization has a culture. Like the tale of the tortoise and the hare, some businesses choose to take a commanding lead in the marketplace, while others prefer to hang back and survey their options more carefully.

A firm's Business Development culture is less clear and less well defined, because most people understand very little about Business Development. Business Development is a term used for everything from sophisticated selling to business growth through mergers and acquisitions.

A Business Development culture is anchored upon either goals or purpose. A goal-driven culture is focused on revenue growth, bookings, stock appreciation and internally focused metrics, primarily intended to drive behavior and desired results.

A purpose-driven culture is focused upon understanding the problems and issues experienced by your market, your customers and, most importantly, the individuals who purchase your products and services. A purpose-driven culture focuses on how to provide solutions to prospect problems, whether or not there is an immediate purchase or an immediate revenue result to the firm.

Given the benefits and risks, can a balance exist between a purpose-driven and a goal-driven Business Development culture? Yes, and ideally that balance should be present. The resulting culture also requires the buy-in/ownership of all within the organization engaged in customer contact. If personnel exhibit conflicting Business Development cultures, the inconsistency causes confusion in the marketplace. This will tend to seriously erode the overall client/prospect confidence in a company, weaken competitive advantage and dissolve any hard-earned trust. No firm can afford to let that happen.

Revenue generation derives from the trust-based relationships produced by a strong, consistent and well-balanced Business Development culture.

So what is your Business Development culture?

#3

Digging the Business Development Ditch...Are You Turning It Around or Digging Deeper?

Do you constantly struggle to reach growth targets or achieve revenue quotas? Does it seem like you're sinking deeper into a ditch, while working hard to climb your way out? Turning around an average or sub-standard Business Development organization requires that you stop doing the same thing with the same people while expecting different results.

Every year threatens to be a tougher business climate for revenue growth. Given this information, it's going to be harder to close deals and win business with greater competition vying for limited opportunities. Average performers will not make an impact in this climate. Have you evaluated your team in preparation for this change? If not, now is the time to do it.

We are often asked to assist companies by performing an objective third-party view of their Business Development organization. Over the years we have found three key items that can affect change in almost any organization. The bottom line with making any permanent change in the behavior of a team is to change not only individual thinking, but also to collectively change the organizational culture. To do this there needs to be a strategic realignment of Business Development planning, process and personnel (the 3 Ps).

Planning

Planning is the first step in any restructuring. Be careful not to confuse a laundry list of objectives with a well-developed operational and tactical Business Development plan.

Process

Process drives behavior; without a solid, customized Business Development process, which your team not only buys into but uses, you might as well aim low and continue digging.

Personnel

Ultimately, without people capable of closing the deal, you will never achieve your goals. The personnel area covers two critical components, leadership and staff.

Without leaders who can integrate or turn around a Business Development organization, you will battle to make the transformation. You need to understand both the mechanical and conceptual limitations that may be hindering your team's success in developing business. A good leader knows how to overcome these limitations and understands when to cut loose those individuals who will never make any changes.

Successful Business Development organizations master these critical components and keep them in alignment. Without a Business Development plan—along with clear leadership and direction on how to execute it—and motivated, capable personnel, you will never climb out of the ditch. Stop digging. Take a hard look at your situation and then make a determination about whether or not you are moving in the right direction.

With a good, objective understanding of your organization's present state, you will be able to recognize the challenges, address the shortcomings and strategically align plans, process and personnel to be prepared for whatever the future brings.

#4
Success in Business Development Depends on 3 Ps.

In working with a wide variety of organizations across different markets, we have found that the Business Development challenges that organizations experience generally relate to the 3 Ps (planning, process and personnel). It might surprise you how many organizations inhibit revenue growth by not focusing on these 3 critical areas. Plans provide the vision and strategy to get where you need to go. Process ensures repeatability and consistency in how clients are engaged, opportunities are identified, qualified and captured and how compliant proposals are written. People are the "doers." Without them you have nothing.

Each of the 3 Ps is equally critical to an organization's long-term Business Development success. Without good plans, a proactive Opportunity Identification and Qualification (OI&Q)[i] Phase and Client Engagement Process, even the best Business Development personnel will struggle in their role. Personality-driven Business Development organizations are generally the result of weak or non-existent plans and process. Business Development superstars often emerge as the "white knights" within these organizations. However, with no repeatable or transferable methodology, the organization runs a great risk should they leave. The reverse is also true. Without good people, regardless of how good the plans and processes are, the organization will struggle.

Long-term success in Business Development depends on the 3 Ps: plans, people and process. Without all three, your revenue generation capability is most likely ineffective.

#5
Principles, Purpose and Process

Professionals in Business Development understand the interrelationship among principles, purpose and process. In your initial contact with potential clients, here are the first three things they want to know:

1) Are you a principle-centered individual? What are your principles for business and business relationships?

2) What is your purpose for contacting them?

3) What is your process for engaging them?

Be anchored in your principles, able to articulate your purpose and use a clearly defined process. Articulating your principles and your purpose should always precede the implementation of your Business Development process.

The key to being a true Business Development Professional is to understand your value, as your company's representative, in the transaction. The key ingredient is you ... your principles, your purpose and your ability to help the client resolve their issues and concerns and negotiate a comfortable win-win process. This position differentiates you from others in the marketplace, and it helps you differentiate your products and services from your competitors.

#6

Business Development Is Hysterical Activity on the Way to the Grave; It Is Not Relevant Social Behavior.

Do you find yourself taking your role as a Business Development Professional too seriously? Over the many years we've been helping students differentiate between and prioritize self-identity and role-identity, it still surprises us how many students continue to place their professional role at the top of their priority list. While your role-identity as a Business Development Professional generates revenue and provides financial security for you and your family, it's simply not the most important role you play. It's just one of the many roles you play in your life ... true? To break it down, your professional role affords you the daily opportunity to help other people, learn new and interesting things, receive financial reward, and, if you choose, the opportunity to have fun!

In the greater scheme of life and in light of our mission, Business Development is really hysterical activity. Those of us who've been in the role for any length of time have lived through more human behavior stories than could be found in the most colorful *New York Times* bestseller. Quite honestly, Business Development is not activity that often engenders the most relevant social behavior. Look at your daily behaviors. Consider the questions you ask, the behavior you exhibit, your ability to engage other people, and your ability to work from their perspective. These are not the behaviors you would expect to be exhibited by the typical Business Development Professional.

To be even more successful in Business Development, lighten up, enjoy the journey, learn from your prospects and learn from your experiences. As a professional Business Developer, don't take yourself or any situation too seriously, and always be thankful for your resulting opportunities.

2

CHAPTER TWO:

Goal Setting and Planning Insights

The following six insights cover Goal Setting and Planning. Without goals and plans, you will struggle to be successful as a Business Development Professional.

#7

Always Have a Goal; Activity Is Not Accomplishment.

Do your homework the first time and on every call. Focus your research around the 4 Cornerstones of Business Development: *Technical, Business, Money* and *People Knowledge*. Pay special attention to People Psychology knowledge: what has changed about the individual and their situation, and what additional individuals should you be contacting to secure this business?

For the first call and every call—always have a goal. Know where you are in your system, where you are starting from and what you have to do to accomplish the goal. Remember, activity is not accomplishment. Know your questions, process, and objectives on every call.

#8

You Must Pick the Role, Set the Goal and Be Willing to Pay the Toll.

To thrive in the "new normal" of Business Development, every component of your individual Business Development process must be both efficient and effective. What may have enabled you to win opportunities in the past may no longer be working. Now is the time to take stock and to do a personal review to ensure your roles and goals are still aligned.

Roles

"Roles are what you do. Self is who you are.."

As you evaluate your current role, perform a personal SWOT analysis: what are your **S**trengths, **W**eaknesses, **O**pportunities and **T**hreats? Develop a good understanding of whether you are a Business Development specialist or generalist. Are you just identifying and qualifying opportunities, or are you responsible for all the components including generating the proposal? Be sure that your current role is aligned not only with your strengths, but also with your goals.

Goals

"Personal and professional. They are different."

The best people in Business Development are goal-driven, self-managed professionals. They have both short and long-term personal and professional goals and plans. Without goals and plans, it is very difficult to evaluate your present or future positions. How else can you measure whether or not your current position is assisting you in getting where you want to go in both your personal and professional life? If you don't have goals, it's a good time to sit down and go through a Goal Setting and Planning exercise.

Tolls

"There is no free lunch. Success in any role in life requires a toll to be paid. Be prepared to pay full price one time."

Once you have completed the role and goal assessment, and you are convinced that your current role is a good fit for both your strengths and future ambitions, then it's time to put together the implementation plan. Work out what additional skills or resources you need to meet your goals and make the financial or time investment to acquire them. Paying the toll also relates to the on-the-job time investment you make to succeed in the role.

Winning business in the current environment requires significant adjustment from the way you won business in the past. "If you are in a hole, you need to stop digging and take a look around. Business Development has been an easy role for many in the past, but things have changed dramatically. The days of easy money will not be back anytime soon. Now is the time to ensure you are in the right role, one that is aligned with and will help you achieve your personal goals. Once these are in alignment, then *pay the toll once* and make every effort to guarantee your personal success.

#9

Don't Put Your Future in Someone Else's Hands.

Future revenue growth requires planning, process and hard work. In order to be successful, you need to take control of your destiny. Many companies that rely heavily on outside influence for their growth during good times will struggle to survive in a downturn. Two examples of this might be:

1. Responding to Requests for Proposal (RFPs) where the customer may never have been engaged and starting their acquisition process at the point of RFP release.
2. Relying on a good proposal to influence the source selection board.

Some companies take a different approach. They focus on working with clients early in their buying process to identify opportunities. As a result, these firms continue to be successful in any environment. They continue to engage customers early to develop a real understanding of their needs and work with them to define the solution. These organizations decide to control their own destiny instead of waiting for the release of a perfect "blue bird" opportunity.

As you confront the "new normal" of business acquisition in any industry, you have the power to master your own destiny by proactively engaging customers, identifying their issues and shaping their thinking as it relates to a solution. The alternative is to wait until the RFP is released, write what you believe is a winning proposal and then put your faith in the hands of the source selection committee. If option #2 is your strategy, be warned ... if you have not influenced the solution, your competition probably has!

#10

Goals Must Come from Our Core.

Much has been written about motivation, and experts agree that effective motivation is ultimately self-motivation. We are motivated to either avoid a pain or pursue a pleasure. Motivation can either be negative in the short-term (e.g., the fear of losing a job, loss of income, disappointment, etc.) or positive in the long-term with the aim of achieving a goal that's been set. Self-sustaining motivation has to be internal and long-term which is exhibited in the goals and plans you set for yourself.

People who perceive themselves in control of their own fate are, in fact, self-motivated. They are more likely to feel in control when stressors affect them. Instead of blaming external sources, they use motivation to look for a solution to deal with the problem. This positive behavior helps in achieving goals and finding personal contentment and professional success.

Motivation in its simplest form is the ability to imagine the future and to plan the action required to achieve it. It allows you to put a plan into action, helps prepare you to pay full price every day and tracks your progress towards the goal. In *Winning Conversations: Mastering the Art of Business Development*, we discuss the Motivation Formula: Motivation = D (Dissatisfaction in your present state) + A (Awareness of the desired result, expectation or vision you have for yourself) + K (Knowledge of a plan on how to get there). One of the key components in mastering the Business Development process is successful Goal

Setting and Planning. These critical components provide self-motivation, which is necessary to sustain ourselves through challenges and to force us to be decision makers.

The mistake often made is to look outside of ourselves for goal setting: "What goal should I aim for?" This approach does not work. True motivation cannot be faked or found externally. It is only when our goals come from the core of our being that are we fully involved in achieving them.

#11
Goal Power: All Motivation Is Ultimately Self-Motivation.

It has been mentioned before that all motivation is self-motivation. But, this time we'll focus on the power that goals have as a motivation catalyst. More than most fields, Business Development is a self-managing profession driven by goals, not controls. Goals become a tangible expression of what motivates a Business Development Professional. It's surprising how often individuals charged with Business Development do not realize that goal setting and subsequent goal achievement are the most important characteristics of their success in this role.

This goal setting stuff may sound a bit naïve, but we've seen the powerful results of simple goal setting exercises. We strongly believe that personal and professional Goal Setting and Planning are integral building blocks for Business Development effectiveness. This experience has helped many of our clients become decision makers, making better decisions professionally and personally through goal setting in both of these areas.

From our considerable experience in directing effective Business Development teams, we've learned that both personal and organizational goals and plans must exist and be aligned to permit a synergistic mix for team success. Now is the optimum time to re-examine your progress on your own personal and professional goals and realign accordingly. It's never too late to proactively establish well defined goals that are congruent with your company's mission and that are well aligned with your personal roles. Without goals, a life isn't lived to its fullest. Goals provide the motivation to make this possible.

#12

Any Strength to an Extreme Becomes a Weakness.

One of the components of successful Goal Setting and Planning is to help identify your personal strengths and weaknesses. We use this exercise to identify weaknesses and put together action plans to offset those shortcomings. Few of us realize that sometimes our strengths can lead to weakness. In the case where a strength taken to an extreme becomes a weakness, we may become too focused, too committed, too articulate or too polished in our Business Development process.

The late John Wooden, the legendary UCLA basketball coach, provided us a good example of this concept in the context of competitiveness. In his experience, he saw that being too competitive caused an individual to lose self-control and become tight emotionally, mentally, and physically. Instead of being too competitive and overly worried about the final score, he constantly urged his players, "to strive for the self-satisfaction that always comes from knowing you did the best you could to become the best of which you are capable." For us, this means putting your efforts into developing yourself across the board. Concentrate on those areas you identified as needing attention and quit relying exclusively upon your well developed, and perhaps, overused strong points.

Any strength you take to an extreme will become your weakness. Discover what you are really good at, and then ask yourself if you unknowingly overplay that strong point to the detriment of everything else.

If you focus only on your strengths, you may be short-changing the areas that you really need to focus upon to better yourself.

3

CHAPTER THREE:

Business Development Role Insights

The following four insights focus on the Business Development role. One of the most critical factors for success in professional Business Development is the ability to separate ourselves from our roles—the ability to distinguish who we are from what we do.

#13

Are You a Strategic Business Leader?

Many individuals who claim the Strategic Business Leader title bring working, personal relationships with the senior management of prospect organizations to their firms. There are a lot of individuals with this basic profile who declare they are strategic Business Development Professionals. However, in reality, they are not.

To be a true Strategic Business Leader who is innovative, creative, and successful, you must be able to innately apply the following seven critical concepts.

First, you must exhibit the hunter profile, always pursuing the best strategic opportunities for your company and crafting those opportunities before competitors recognize them.

Second, it's critical that you understand the goal and purpose of Business Development. You should understand that the purpose of your role is to help organizations understand their real issues, challenges or concerns, and identify their pain.

Third, you must have a developed knowledge of psychology, understanding how and why people behave the way they do. The application of people knowledge is what motivates a prospect to trust an individual and share information.

The fourth concept is the capacity to develop the behavioral characteristics of an intelligence gatherer. This is the critical ability to know what information is important to gather early on, and then who to gather it from, and how.

The fifth important trait of the Strategic Business Leader is the ability and courage to disqualify opportunities early and efficiently. That means letting go of bad opportunities, walking away and moving on to a better opportunity.

The sixth must-have is the skill to quickly build both a short and long-term pipeline. To do this you must have the appropriate character, develop and hone the right thinking and be educated or re-educated in the role of professional Business Development.

The last quality is the ego drive to continually pursue new opportunities as an alpha wolf. With their heightened sixth sense, alpha wolves have the ability to see leverage points and make connections that others fail to make.

Are Strategic Business Leaders born with the Business Development gene, or can they be developed in this role? From our years in this business, the simple answer is that it's a little of both. Few bring it all. That's where professional development and mastery education come into the strategic Business Development equation.

Are you a Strategic Business Leader?

#14

Fishing versus Catching, Hunting versus Bagging

Early American pioneers quickly learned that if you didn't hunt and fish, you wouldn't eat. The same is true for Business Development Professionals. Individuals may see themselves as pioneers in their organizations, exploring new markets or searching for new opportunities. However, there are many folks in Business Development roles who have never learned to be self-sufficient. They've been a part of an industry or organization where strong demand exists and market position is so dominant, that business develops itself and order-taking is the rule of the day.

Unfortunately this rarely lasts, as markets mature and competition appears. But frequently, the mindset or culture remains. Business Development personnel begin to believe that a "job fairy" makes visits on a regular basis, and they wait in eager anticipation for the next deal or project to appear. Many organizations and Business Development individuals have found themselves in serious financial straits relying on business they didn't generate.

The hunter or fisher mind-set is a learned mentality of the "intrepreneurial" Business Development Professional. They've learned the thinking, discipline and process of proactively producing business. These professionals learned that to eat, they must know how to hunt and fish, regardless of conditions.

However, not every day in the field or on the water will bring success. The same is true for Business Development. Not every call will produce a prospect or a sale. If it did, we'd call it catching and bagging, not hunting and fishing.

Working hard and smart every day to proactively generate business on your own makes you a better revenue producer. The lessons learned, relationships developed and problems solved make for a day well spent and a career well served.

Be proactive and self-sufficient. Learn to hunt and fish. You'll learn a lot about yourself ... and you might just help the economy too!

#15
It's Easier to Find a Diamond in the Rough Than It Is to Apply Pressure to Coal.

From our experience working with Business Development Professionals, two challenges consistently arise. First, it is extremely difficult to change the behavior and thinking of traditional sales people who are typically product-oriented and who push-sell based on the features, benefits and pricing of their product. It is true that any system will work as long as you have one. That system of continually pushing the value and service of the product, although inefficient and ineffective, will generate a certain amount of business. However, it will almost always put the individual representing the product in an adversarial role.

Helping a person to recognize the limitations of that system, changing the thinking that drives it and elevating them to the higher level of Business Development has a low probability of success and is a painfully difficult process.

Secondly, individuals who are by nature problem solvers—introspective, somewhat introverted, interested in asking questions and learning, empathetic and able to understand a problem from another person's perspective—make much better candidates for developing into Business Development Professionals. What sets them apart is their desire to understand the nature and scope of the problem, its ramifications to both the individual and the purchasing organization and being externally focused in helping to find a solution to the problem—whether or not the prospect purchases it from them. This type of individual engenders a more open relationship with strengthened trust and a superior exchange of information, resulting in a longer lasting professional business relationship.

In the modern world of service-oriented, technical services companies, a technical engineering specialist who has backed into the role of Business Development provides a much better candidate for success, is a more reflective student, and is more inclined to learn both the thinking and process of professional Business Development than a traditional salesperson.

It is much easier to discover a diamond in the rough and to mentor and coach this individual rather than to try to retrain traditional sales thinking and process.

★ ★ ★

#16
Shapers, Fakers and Order-Takers

Few positions have the success of an organization weighing on them like Business Development positions. An extensive investment is often required to onboard a new Business Development hire. Once a hiring decision is made, an even more substantial time and financial investment is required to allow the individual to develop relationships and begin qualifying and shaping opportunities. This investment may continue for many years. It's no wonder why hiring teams often feel like they are looking for a diamond in the rough.

Understanding how a Business Development candidate will perform in the role is critical and often hard to determine. Business Development personnel will fit into one of the three categories below, whether or not they (or you) realize it. Understanding where your potential new hire fits into these categories is imperative to their success in their Business Development role, and consequently, your ROI.

Shapers

Early shapers are revenue makers. Shapers proactively engage with clients and ethically work to craft requirements in their organizations' best interest. Shaping is not a new concept and has been the focus of great Business Development people for years. However, very few individuals have taken the time to learn how to shape the opportunity during the early Opportunity Identification and Qualification (OI&Q)[i] Phase. Shapers are proactive in gathering intelligence early and working with the prospect to shape opportunities.

Fakers

Beware of the fakers. These individuals have great looking resumes complete with glowing accolades. But, begin asking them tough questions and you will quickly find that they show a lot of activity, but never close the deal. Fakers are often hard to detect until an organization has already invested considerable revenue and time in pursuing opportunities. They know everything about the opportunity, but they've had limited substantive interfacing with any prospects. At that point, it becomes increasingly hard to cut the loss. These individuals are good at finding the next "great" opportunity, they "drink their own bathwater," spin the data, and really believe what they have is valid. What you discover is that they seldom develop any high value human Intel that allows for making unbiased, critical pursue/no-pursue decisions.

Order-Takers

Depending on their role, order-takers can either be a great asset or a tremendous liability. In a primary Business Development role they are a disaster, preferring to stay in the office waiting for the customer to call and often busying themselves with administrative tasks to avoid engaging clients. Good order-takers are great when they proactively expand the current projects by harvesting additional revenue. These types of individuals pay the overhead, but in a changing business environment, they struggle to achieve continued revenue growth.

As you recruit your next Business Development Professional, make sure you know how to separate the shapers, fakers and order-takers.

4

CHAPTER FOUR:

Self-Worth Insights

The next five insights cover an individual's self-worth. Highly successful Business Development Professionals understand the value they bring to the client and understand that the Business Development role does not impact their self-worth—it is just a role.

#17
Know Your Value: Your Purpose Statement

Leadership in Business Development is about character. Being a leader, rising to the top 3% in your profession, is anchored on your principles, ethics and values. Your purpose—what you do for other people—evolves out of these principles, ethics and values.

The purpose of a professional in Business Development is to help prospects or clients identify their issues or concerns and help them find a way to solve them, whether or not they purchase from you. Your purpose is what adds intrinsic value to the relationship. Your character and principles are measured in every contact early on, through your purpose statement. How well you clearly articulate your purpose is a reflection on you as a professional and a leader in Business Development.

#18
Know That You Have Value in the Relationship.

The distinguishing factor in many Business Development situations is you as an individual. Know yourself, your principles, your purpose, your values and your ethics. Have confidence in your process. Realize that you bring immeasurable value to the relationship. Your purpose—determining what the client needs and helping them get it whether or not they obtain it from you—differentiates your company, your services, and your relationships from those of your competitors.

#19

Who You Call On Is a Reflection of How You See Yourself.

In your life roles you receive treatment that is consistent with your level of thinking. One of the keys to success in Business Development is understanding how your thinking impacts your role behavior. Most of us have been programmed to think in a manner consistent with what other people have established as role expectations. Changing this programmed thinking/role expectation is challenging. The objective is to learn to think like an "intrepreneurial" business person. You are challenged to see yourself and think like the CEO of "You, LLC." You are your best product.

In our Business Development education programs, we engage in an exercise to help people understand that role performance, in any role in life, is tied to how they have been programmed to see themselves (i.e. self-perception). Similarly, the level or status of the role they are in is quite often formed by how they have seen themselves in previous roles. One of the interesting things we've found is that an individual's level of thinking tends to constrain role advancement.

If you have a tendency not to get to the decision maker, that's a pretty good sign that you still have some problems with self versus role in Business Development. Instead of seeing yourself as equal to a high level executive or flag officer, you will find yourself filling a subservient role during the interaction. Another manifestation is to avoid calling at the top level in an organization and to prefer calling on those at a level you are comfortable with regardless of whether or not they are decision makers.

In Business Development, it is essential that you learn to think on the same level as the individual you wish to engage. When you get your thinking on an equal basis with your prospect, you will see yourself on an equal basis with your prospect.

Here are five practical steps to begin overcoming this hurdle:

1. Identify the conceptual or psychological limitations that are holding you back. Figure out why you think the way you do and identify the underlying cause. This is conceptual, psychological self-analysis. It's not easy or pretty, but it will change your life.

2. Do your homework. Fear is best overcome with preparation. If you are prepared and have done your homework and research, you will present yourself more credibly to the prospect.

3. Define your purpose. Do you have a defined goal and purpose in Business Development? If so, are you owning your purpose statement and articulating it to your prospects?

4. Be a decision maker. Decision makers like to deal with other decision makers. Complete a personal and professional Goal Setting and Planning exercise or revisit your own personal and professional goals and plans to see if they're in alignment.

5. Challenge yourself to take risks. There is no growth without pain. Make sure you are pursuing success more than you are avoiding failure. You're not growing if you are not psychologically uncomfortable. Remember… no one ever died doing Business Development; some only wish they had.

#20
How You Do in Your Roles in Life Is Not a Reflection of You As an Individual.

Business Development is a role; it is not a value judgment of you as an individual. One of the challenging psychological principles that individuals in Business Development have to accept is the separation of role-identity and self-identity. Individuals who equate role-identity with self-worth are significantly handicapped in the Business Development role. When you understand that Business Development has substantial, recurring and inherent risk, you quickly realize that individuals who equate role success with self-worth are by nature risk adverse and, therefore, struggle in this role.

The ability to accept your Business Development role with its inherent challenges, both personally and professionally, provides an opportunity for growth. Your success or failure in this role and your other roles in life does not make you worth any more or any less as an individual. First and foremost, self-worth is determined by what you believe your worth is. Reaffirming or re-establishing a healthy self-concept is critical for success in the role of Business Development.

All our roles in life have priorities which are different for each of us. As individuals, we all have inherent worth. Once we learn to accept ourselves, like ourselves and value ourselves as individuals, we do well in all of our roles. Role and self are two separate components of you as an individual; they are not one and the same.

Individuals who confuse role-identity with self-identity find it difficult to put themselves in the high risk situations that successful Business Development requires.

#21

Sales Is No Place to Evaluate Your Self-Worth.

Fear of rejection is one of the biggest inhibitors for people in sales and Business Development roles. This is because these individuals equate their Business Development role performance and their self-worth. In doing so, they are inherently risk adverse and extremely cautious in executing a process, reluctant to call on senior level individuals and will avoid pushing decisions if there is the possibility of a no. They do this because they equate the no with failure, not only in the role of Business Development, but also in their personal role as individuals. What these individuals have done is put their self-worth and self-respect on the line along with the sale and, therefore, must close the sale in order to validate their self-worth. Getting a no is a rejection of not only their efforts in Business Development, but a rejection of themselves personally. This negatively impacts not only their self-esteem, but also their ability to perform the role effectively.

Business Development is not a role in which you try to validate your self-worth. You have intrinsic value as a person which is totally separate from your performance in this role. Your success or failure here is a function of your choices in the role, the training you have been fortunate to obtain and the psychological limitations you bring to the role.

5

CHAPTER FIVE:

Risking and Resisting Change Insights

These five insights cover risking and resisting change. This is an area where many of us struggle. Change is never easy. There are some people who embrace it while others resist it at all cost. Business Development Professionals embrace change, understand how to risk and are not afraid of failure.

#22

Everybody Wants to Go to Heaven ... Nobody Wants to Die.

If you really want to be successful in any role in life, especially the role of Business Development, you have to be prepared to pay full price one time. This is true about any role in your life. Most of us are not aware of what "full price" means to truly master a role. It is a life-long journey, both in personal and professional development. In its simplest form, it says that everyone wants the reward ... nobody really wants to do all of the work. A lot of people are what could be considered successful in their roles. They simply can't or won't pay the full price to become the very best in those roles. Most traditional salespeople look, sound and act the same. There isn't much to differentiate them. Those individuals who have paid the full price, made the sacrifices, challenged themselves professionally, improved themselves personally—especially on conceptual and leadership matters—enjoy the fruits of their labor.

This particular insight is not unique to MBD[i]. It has been around for some time. Learn what the full price in a role means and be prepared to pay it one time. Life's journey is about enjoying the day-to-day challenges, accepting them, mastering them and earning the reward.

It's never too late to begin that journey.

#23

When the Pain of Change Is Less Than the Pain You're in ... You Will Change.

This insight is based on Herzberg's Motivation Hygiene Concept, which says that people are more motivated to avoid a negative pain than necessarily to pursue a positive. At some time, all of us have come to realize that motivation first starts with a dissatisfaction with where we are. The degree of that dissatisfaction and the ramifications of the situation generate the pain that you experience. Only as that pain increases over time and circumstances—in relation to the pain that it will take to alleviate the problem and/or to bring about change—are you motivated and pushed to move forward.

There is no growth without pain. Change for the better always requires letting loose of a certain degree of the status quo. You realize then that the pain of moving ahead—the trials, the frustrations, the disappointments and the failures—are always better than the situation you once found yourself in. Change won't begin until you seize the courage and mental discipline to immerse yourself in a certain amount of pain and disappointment concerning where you are in the present.

#24

People Don't Fight Change ... They Fight Being Changed.

Most people would say they advocate change and would agree that a certain variety in life adds excitement and makes things more interesting. Be it the change of the seasons or the change in Business Development opportunities, all of us take to something new. Unfortunately, we tend to bring a lot of our old thinking and ways to these new opportunities. In the modern world change is constant; countless activities that were performed manually for generations before are now automated. The way we communicate has changed radically in the new millennium, and this rate of change is ever accelerating.

People tend to get comfortable with the way they approach relationships. They allow themselves to stay in a psychological and emotional comfort zone, which significantly limits their potential and growth. Complacency is a rut—and that rut is a grave with no end. We seldom encourage other people to challenge us to change. We challenge ourselves to change even less frequently. Only through reevaluating our thinking and how we approach our day-to-day behavior will we be able to capitalize on any new opportunities. Change begins from within, and is seldom initiated until the pain of change is less than the pain we are in.

#25

Defend Your Limitations and, Sure Enough, They're Yours.

We frequently encounter individuals who, when challenged with why they continually do things a certain way, will defend their position and the thinking driving their behavior—even when they know the outcome is inherently limited. Unfortunately, this is a natural tendency in all of us, since we rationalize what we've done regardless of the results obtained.

It is seldom the limitations of our *behavior* that get us into unfavorable situations, but rather the limitations in our *thinking*. It's a natural tendency to believe that the thinking we displayed in a particular situation was correct. The limitations in our thinking hold us prisoner to our present situations. Defending these limitations ensures we are limited in our personal and professional growth. The ability to self-analyze the thinking process driving your behavior, without trying to defend it, allows you to uncover the limitations that are holding you back. It has been said that the combination of ignorance and arrogance is unhealthy. Being unaware of your limitations and/or defending them, is a sure way to inhibit your opportunities in the role of Business Development.

Business Development is a role in which you are challenged on a constant basis to analyze and adjust your thinking and your behavior to move past these limitations.

#26

How Good Are You at Successfully Failing?

The philosophy of risking, failing and learning is one of the most powerful concepts to embrace in furthering yourself personally and professionally. How many times have you decided to change because you are disappointed with the current results your prospects delivered, or with your revenue or profit results, and then backed off when the psychological and/or physical discomfort of the unfamiliar set in? Loosening your hold on the status quo to strive for something better is risky business. It carries the risk of failure.

Risking is the act of letting go—letting go of something you are certain of and reaching out for something you are not sure of, but which you believe is better than what you have. In every risk situation there is an unavoidable loss, something that has to be given up in order to move forward. Success depends more on your willingness to risk than being concerned about what happens if you fail.

When you are unhappy with where you are, you should be willing to risk—risk getting out of your comfort zone and risk failure. Only by risking failure are you likely to succeed in anything. Too many people waste their lives thinking their objective is to succeed, when in reality all they are doing is avoiding failure. Furthermore, in their avoidance of failure, they have blocked their deepest creative forces within that can make their lives fulfilling, exciting and meaningful.

The learning part of failure is quite obvious. Every failure represents a lesson. Every failure adds another level of experiential wisdom. Consider this: the most successful Business Development Professionals have failed more than anyone who is a true failure thought possible. Success and failure are deeply intertwined. As former U.S. Secretary of State and Chairman of the Joint Chiefs of Staff Colin Powell once said, "There are no secrets to success. It is the result of preparation, hard work and learning from failure."

Are you ready to risk failure? Are you prepared to fail your way into success? How good are you at successfully failing?

6

CHAPTER SIX:

Thinking Insights

These seven insights cover the thinking necessary for success in Business Development. Thinking and resulting conceptual limitations are key areas where many Business Development Professionals fail.

#27

Be Careful of Running into Your Own Thinking.

Too many people in the role of Business Development get caught up in the mechanics, the questions, the presentation and the processes. It's certainly important to know what to do and how to do it. But, it's equally and frequently more important to know why you're doing it. Mechanics give you the what, when and how but it's the conceptual that gives you the motivation, discipline and courage.

Conceptually, Business Development is about how you see yourself and develop the thinking necessary for success. To be successful, you need to see yourself as a professional business person; that is, one who takes responsibility for helping your client and helping your company and who, in the end, leaves things better than you found them. Too many of us focus internally rather than externally. It's not about you, or the products or services you provide. It's all about the client. It's about understanding their problems from their perspective and then assisting them in securing the best solution, whether or not they purchase it from you.

A wise Pennsylvania Dutch Business Development manager once shared with me, "Be careful of running into your own thinking." This is a challenge for almost everyone in a Business Development role. We simply can't get our own thinking out of the way so that we can focus on the client. This is most often seen as we make assumptions about what we believe the client is thinking rather than asking a clarifying question. The ability to get control of how you think—the good as well as the obsolete and outdated—is a professional growth process in the role of Business Development. To succeed at the highest level, you must gain a good understanding of both leadership and psychology. First, you need to discipline your own thinking as a leader. Only then will you be prepared to assist your client with figuring out what is best for them from their perspective.

#28

Master Long-Term Thinking Like a Business Person versus Short-Term Thinking Like a Salesperson.

From many years of experience, we know that the top 3%—the true professionals in Business Development—have learned how to change their thinking. Not only have they learned how to think like a professional business person; more importantly, they have learned the thinking and the ethos of a leader.

Thinking like a true Business Development Professional involves a complete understanding of the 12 Core Competencies of Business Development. This way of thinking is substantially different than traditional sales thinking. These individuals understand that first this thinking is all about who they are as individuals and leaders with their principles, their values and their purpose.

This thinking is also about what they know, including technical knowledge, understanding of their customer's business, knowing how to help clients make money and an in-depth understanding of psychology and human behavior. The business person understands that it is much more than simply systems and skills, goals and plans. They have developed long-term, right-brained, strategic thinking in addition to short-term, left-brained, sales thinking. The true business person is well-balanced, mature, competent, and has a long-term focus. They keep the end in mind, which is creating a long-term professional business relationship that transcends the short-term sale.

#29

The Thinking That Got You Here Is Not the Thinking That Will Get You Where You Need to Go!

Changing our thinking is not an easy task. After collecting some life experiences, if we are lucky, we are able to reflect on our past and identify what may be holding us back. Through this reflection, we realize that the thinking that got us where we are is not going to take us much further in our lives. If we are fortunate, we finally realize that the pain of change is going to be less than the pain of staying where we are. We begin to set personal and professional goals, commit to achieving them and start to evaluate the thinking that is necessary to move forward. Only by changing our thinking will we change our behavior.

It is this powerful combination of changed thinking and behavior that precipitates significant growth in our lives.

#30
Thinking Comes Right Before Trouble.

We have all heard that any strength to an extreme is a weakness, although many of us fail to really understand this principle. Knowing our strengths and seeing them as potential limitations, will assist us in avoiding situations that occur due to complacency or over-confidence.

Many of us who engage in Business Development are intellectually capable and, as a result, we are always thinking. It is our nature to wonder about what will happen next and why; to anticipate the next move and then how to react. This over-analyzing becomes a limitation when working in the role of Business Development. The overly-capable, intellectual Business Developer will ascribe meaning, make assumptions and leap to conclusions. This is done rather than taking the time to slow down, engage with the prospect at their pace, ask questions, listen to the answers, and then follow up on replies to gather further clarification. Their thinking has hindered them from truly listening to and focusing on the position of the client.

Invariably, this results in the Business Developer losing control of their process. They are soon in trouble, and they revert to selling.

Over-thinking, over-analyzing, anticipating or "listening with your motor running," are all sure signs that trouble is just ahead. Too much thinking without really listening comes right before trouble

#31

Stay Outside Your Conceptual Comfort Zone.

Use your homework prior to every call to stretch yourself conceptually and mechanically. Find out what you don't know about your client's business. How do they really make money? Who are the individuals in the company you need to force yourself to ask about? Who should you be gathering information from that you are reluctant to engage in an interview?

Stretch your thinking in your homework prior to every call. Use your homework, and you'll stretch the results from the call too.

#32

Where Is Your Thinking Taking You?

It is becoming more evident that to be successful in the current business environment, you have to change the way you engage with your prospects. The Business Development processes and thinking that allowed many companies to do extremely well in the past are no longer working. These acquisition processes were predominantly reactive, waiting for the customer to identify their own needs and package them in an RFP. Many companies who won business during those times would admit they never even engaged in a dialogue with the customer. Winning business in this manner led many to believe that this was the best approach; in order to grow revenue you simply responded to more RFPs than your competitors.

In order to prosper in the changing economy with changing government acquisition policies, limited budgets and other constraints, it is now vital to begin your Business Development efforts early in the customer's buying cycle. Those who engage early and work with the client to assist them in understanding their issues, needs and wants will continually win more business than those waiting for an RFP before utilizing their "proposal shop" to write another dazzling proposal.

Winners these days are those who plan their strategy, put in the hard work to assist their potential customers early and do as much as they can to ethically secure the win. You cannot force a person to buy, but you can improve your chances by gaining their trust and assisting them in understanding their issues and the available solutions (yours and others). This is the primary difference between a Business Development approach and a traditional sales approach. One focuses on identifying the prospect's underlying needs and utilizes the skills and experience of the Business Developer to identify or develop the best solution. Traditional push-selling focuses less on the identification of needs and more on pushing a solution and then overcoming the client objections to that solution.

#33

If Your Head Doesn't Get There First, Your Tail Never Will.

For any professional development or transformation of behavior to be effective, you have to change thinking. It's thinking that drives behavior, which drives results. In order to be successful in Business Development, you have to understand the difference between strategic level thinking and tactical or transactional relationships.

Many traditional salespeople get caught in the trap of traditional, transactional selling. Using other questioning techniques, more probes, reversals or mechanics will not substantially change the outcome of that transactional relationship.

In order for individuals to rise to the top 3% in the Business Development role, they must learn how to think at the strategic level, realize what long-term value they bring to the relationship, and partner with their customer or client. People are treated consistent with their level of thinking. In order to relate to senior level decision makers you must learn how to think like a senior level decision maker.

In order to develop a strategic relationship at the executive level, you must transform your thinking to that level ... and the rest of you will follow.

7

CHAPTER SEVEN:

Business Development Relationship Insights

These four insights cover the Business Development relationship. These insights address the relationship between the prospect or client and the Business Development Professional.

#34

Bad Business Is Worse Than No Business.

One lesson a Business Development Professional learns over time is the cost of bad business. Early in our careers, we are so anxious for business that we fail to establish relationship guidelines, which results in bad business relationships. This failure to set the rules and to evaluate the actual cost of a bad, long-term business relationship leads to trouble. If we're lucky, we generate some revenue and commission, and perhaps some profit, all the while rationalizing that at least we have business. Unfortunately, the full cost of bad business is never calculated. We remain in a dependent state of mind, believing that what we have is all we deserve. This makes us vulnerable to taking on additional bad business.

As we gain experience in our careers, we begin to develop some positive, long-term, professional business relationships that benefit both parties. These relationships are based on mutual respect and professionalism, where both parties help each other as well as those beyond the immediate relationship. By comparing these relationships to ones earlier in our careers, we realize that bad business really is worse than no business at all. Bad business often holds us back. We take comfort in believing we have business; however, it's not the kind of business that makes us successful! On the contrary, if you don't have any business, you work hard to find some. It's time to review your opportunities, get rid of the bad business and become excited about finding the good!

★ ★ ★

#35

Your Meter Is Always Running.
It's Always a Business Relationship.

People in Business Development frequently have problems separating business from personal relationships. They think if they develop a personal relationship with a prospect or client, it will enhance their ability to develop business. Unfortunately, once you develop a personal relationship, you lose perspective. You begin to see things from a personal perspective rather than a business perspective. Be professionally involved but emotionally detached.

If you are more interested in maintaining personal relationships than serving clients' needs and solving their problems, you lose your professional, objective perspective, and you cease to be of value to your clients. Prospects or clients deserve the courtesy of being able to honestly evaluate you on a professional, business basis. They should not be encumbered by personal situations or personal involvement with you. Be careful of crossing the fine line from business to personal. You are always on stage with your prospect.

If you don't know if you're on stage ... you're on stage.

#36

Good Matters Get Better. Bad Matters Get Worse.

In Business Development, it's easier to *stay* out of trouble than to *get* out of trouble. What you do to establish the rules of the relationship up front is critical for setting the tone for the relationship. Good relationships in Business Development are typically the result of bonding, mutual trust and respect and agreement on the Rules, Rights and Responsibilities of the working relationship. These relationships lead to long-term, multi-year partnerships that benefit both parties. Business relationships that start without clearly establishing the rules often develop into challenging situations that tend to have an underlying degree of uncertainty or lack of an anchor. They seldom blossom into long-term relationships that can benefit both organizations.

Our experience coaching professionals in their Business Development relationships indicates that if the relationship starts well, the work, effort, and resources invested in it will almost always yield a positive return. This is true whether executing a single Business Development process or looking at a long-term relationship. Situations that start off on the wrong foot, awkwardly and incompletely, inevitably get worse over time. At best, the additional effort invested in these marginal relationships seldom return above average results. Take any situation you encounter and scale it on a level of 0 to 10. If a situation starts at a 6 or above, it can turn out to be outstanding with continued hard work. When a relationship starts at a 2, 3 or 4, the best result you will ever get with a considerable amount of effort is a 6 or 7.

Good matters get better, bad matters inevitably get worse.

#37
Every Day You Do Business with Someone, You Are One Day Closer to Ending It.

This insight is often misunderstood and can be confusing if you don't understand the principle behind it. We all assume that once we have worked hard and won the client's trust, they are ours forever. In our arrogance, we believe they are loyal and appreciative of what we provide them and are never vulnerable to the competition.

Professionals in Business Development understand that their job is to help prospects uncover problems, help them to recognize these challenges and assist them in finding solutions, whether they purchase them from us or not. Should you be fortunate enough to win trust, respect and business from a customer, your responsibility is to provide solutions to their problems as quickly as possible. Here is a paradox to consider: work hard to work yourself out of business, and clients will give you more business.

If you make the mistake of assuming that your client owes you business, based on the past relationship, you are one day closer to losing the client. Past clients owe you nothing! Every day is a new day in Business Development. You earn your business on each call and with each situation. It is the client's unilateral privilege to extend the relationship to you, which allows you to be in the preferred position for future business.

8

CHAPTER EIGHT:

Business Development Process Insights

These six insights cover Business Development process. Having, understanding and using a Business Development process is critical. If you are not using one, then you can be certain you are part of someone else's process.

#38

A Good Business Development System Forces You to Get Noes Early and Often.

Many traditional sales processes are push-oriented and focused on features and benefits. These processes attempt to convince prospects that they need products or services. This methodology is based on the premise that if there is a need, prospects should say yes by acknowledging their need and buying the product or service. Very few, if any, sales processes operate from the premise that people buy for their reasons and never yours. Just because you have it, doesn't mean they need it!

A good Business Development process disqualifies unqualified opportunities early and often. It is set up to disqualify individuals early if there are no problems that can be solved, if there is no budget, or if the individuals are not prepared to invest funds to solve the problems. Getting noes early and often, valuing the noes, and understanding that by successfully disqualifying unqualified situations quickly, you are then free to invest your time dealing with valuable prospects who need and are willing to purchase your products or services.

Learn the value of noes. Encourage your prospects to disqualify themselves early, saving valuable time and effort in determining whether or not you can benefit each other.

#39
The Key to Business Development Is Learning What Pains You Solve.

Learning what pains you solve in Business Development begins with an understanding of how and why people buy. Unfortunately, most of us fail to understand what ultimately motivates the buyer's decision making process. Specifically, we fail to discipline ourselves in our process to learn from the prospect's perspective what real problems and issues we solve for them. This means looking beyond the described symptoms and digging down to the real problem, which is often disguised or hidden. In Business Development we refer to this as "The Principle of the First Cause." The frustrations at the top of the prospect's worry list are usually the first-person, personal pains which point to the First Cause.

To be effective, we must learn to think from the prospect's perspective. We need to ask hard questions to uncover their pains or concerns that will be addressed by purchasing from us. Learn to understand and focus on what pain looks like from your prospect's point of view. If you focus on the pains which are extracting an emotional toll from your prospect, you will be able to bond and position at the right level with them, allowing you to qualify efficiently and effectively within your Business Development process.

Your purpose is to take things off your client's worry list.

#40

If You Don't Already Know By Bid Day Who Won the Bid … It Probably Isn't You

When responding to bids or RFPs there is a key point to understand: you are automatically a part of someone else's process. That may be either the prospect's process or a competitor's bid-shaping process. Either way, what you think is an open opportunity is actually a situation where the prospect has already determined their issues, decided they want to address them, allocated some of their budget and launched a decision making process. In essence, they have self-qualified. They have worked their own process or have been a part of someone else's bid-shaping process, and you are now responsive, reactive and dependent.

In this situation, you have very little leverage for gathering quality information, much less high-value human Intel that affords you an advantage in submitting a bid.

The key to being successful in responding to RFPs is to have an Opportunity Identification and Qualification (OI&Q)[i] Phase that allows you to engage key individuals early on. You must help uncover their issues, shape their perspective of their situation and, more importantly, shape their vision of the solution. Employing an identification and qualification phase in your Business Development process allows you to be integral in defining what will be in a final RFP. If you aren't engaged early in an acquisition process, it's unlikely that what you receive in the bid documentation will articulate well the key issues to which you can respond effectively.

Keep in mind the 60/40 rule: 60% of the work in developing an opportunity is done up-front, before any RFP or proposal is ever drafted. The purpose of the proposal is to be able to address the specific problems the client understands they have and are motivated to solve. If the proposal is tailored towards the issues which you have helped the client define and become motivated to solve, then you have a decided advantage in the bid situation, regardless of the competition.

Seldom are bids won on the scope of work or competitiveness of the price. It is the relationship that is developed up front, the prospect's trust and respect and their desire to work specifically with you that gives you a definite edge in an RFP. If you don't ensure early on that you are the prospect's preferred source for a solution, you need to realize that your competition is more likely to win the business than you are.

The bottom line is: if you don't know by bid day who won the bid, it probably isn't you.

#41

Do You See "No" As the End or the Beginning?

One of the defining characteristics between amateurs and Business Development Professionals is their early pursuit of "no." Business Development professionals have moved beyond fearing rejection and understand that getting a no is a healthy part of the Business Development process. They also understand the value associated with a no.

When you reach an impasse in uncovering additional issues or moving a client to a decision point, it's time to disengage professionally, tactfully and appropriately. This is the time you nurture the client in an appropriate manner asking that they say no to further discussions. Doing so will benefit everyone.

Once you get the no, you ask yourself, "Should I leave, or should I begin the real interview?" The professional begins where the amateur bails out. It's as easy as asking, "Now that we've come to this point, would you be kind enough to give me a lesson?" By continuing the discussion and asking the right questions, you gain valuable insight on how to refine your dialogue with prospects and improve the efficiency and effectiveness of your qualification process.

Be aware that you paid for this lesson with your time commitment and your purpose in trying to help the client. If you're not smart enough to take the trip to no and get beyond it to secure the lesson, it's your loss. There is great benefit in performing Business Development autopsies, discovering where things didn't work out, getting to no early and then moving beyond it. More often than not, you may find this is an opportunity to move ahead with the client on a different course.

The ability to move beyond the amateur to the professional depends on the lessons learned after you've solicited noes.

#42
Only Decision Makers Can Discuss Money.

This insight has implications for both the Business Development Professional as well as the prospect. If you are not a decision maker you will have a hard time bringing up and discussing money. Only you as a decision maker will be comfortable bringing up and expecting to discuss financial issues. This stumbling block is most frequently a conceptual problem. Injecting your own personal thinking and feelings about money into your Business Development process is deadly.

The second part of this insight relates to your prospects. You can quickly determine the level of thinking and decision making ability of individuals you are engaged with by asking questions about money. Decision makers within an organization have knowledge of budgets, access to funds and authority to spend. By discussing the money step early and learning to be comfortable asking forthright questions about money, you can quickly determine whether or not your prospects are significant decision makers.

Ultimately, only decision makers can legitimately discuss financial investments.

#43

The 3 Cs (Credibility, Confidence and Courage) = Success in Business Development

Credibility, confidence and courage are three interwoven factors essential for Business Development success. These key elements make us powerful, efficient and effective in the role. Any one of these attributes is powerful by itself. Put together, they provide a formidable advantage for the Business Development Professional.

Credibility is the value we see in ourselves in helping others with their challenges. This is different from relying on our product's features and benefits or company's name brand. It is uniquely what you as an individual bring to the table in understanding the prospect's pain and helping them find a solution. The knowledge that you are able to help others solve their problems puts you in a profoundly powerful position.

After hours of study, practice and learning from our mistakes, we have confidence in executing our Business Development process. We know what to do, how to do it and why it works.

As professionals, we are anchored in the principles and values that give us courage to do what's right for the client. Courage comes from having total confidence in our Business Development process. We put our purpose (helping prospects discover what their problems are and finding solutions—whether or not they purchase from us), before our goal of making a sale. We know it's the right thing to do in building a long-term relationship.

9

CHAPTER NINE:

Client Engagement Insights

Ultimately, Business Development is all about Client Engagement and your ability to gain trust, confidence and information. These fourteen insights address how a Business Development Professional approaches and engages with clients and prospects.

#44

Don't Look Too Good or Talk Too Wise.

In his poem "If", Rudyard Kipling shares examples on how to relate to others and exhibit grace, class and humility. People are comfortable with and instinctively trust those individuals who they sense are much like themselves. We've learned from our work in psychology that clients want and need to feel OK. When we come across more OK than our clients, either intentionally or unintentionally, we create a barrier to trust and buying.

Look good, but not too good. Talk wisely, but not too wisely. Always allow the prospect the chance to look and feel a little superior to you. It helps their ego, and it allows you the opportunity to build trust and gain entry into their world, their ideas, their issues and their buying motivations.

#45

There Are No Customers Who Do Not Buy, but Simply Prospects Who Fail to Qualify.

Many people in sales and Business Development believe the reason a prospect didn't buy is that they lacked sufficient information, enough justification or adequate incentives convincing them to buy. This is an example of a traditional push-sell philosophy and the peddler mentality.

In reality, the Business Development Professional quickly recognizes that this prospect failed to qualify for their product or service. Either they didn't have pain, weren't aware of it and motivated to do something about it, or other significant conditions were present that should have disqualified them earlier in the process. Prospects cannot be expected nor pushed to buy a product or service that they do not see addressing an issue of significance to them at that particular time.

It is not our sales ability as professionals that win us business. What makes the sale is our skill to quickly and efficiently qualify prospects that have the motivation and means to purchase our products and services.

#46

In Business Development, Stay Professionally Involved But Emotionally Detached.

Along with your purpose in Business Development, your ability to stay emotionally detached in interactions with prospects and clients is a critical component to your success. Emotion impacts both ends of the transaction: don't expect a prospect/client to be concerned about your feelings; and in turn, do be objective in assessing the relationship in order to do what's best for your prospect or client.

In reality, this is easier said than done. Even though we are aware that Business Development isn't the role where we get our emotional needs met, we still fall into the trap of relating the closing of a deal to personal and professional self-worth. This is a no-win scenario. Allowing feelings to interfere in the transaction seriously damages your ability to fulfill your purpose—doing what's in the client's best interest.

In Business Development, it's never about you. It's all about the client and their needs, their concerns, their perspective on the problem and, ultimately, their decision about the solution. In some cases, the solution may not even involve you or your company!

Professional objectivity is key to establishing trust and credibility in any long-term Business Development relationship. Leaving emotion out of the transaction is the best way to achieve it.

#47
Work on the Right Side of the Problem.

Often, when we encounter problems in the role of Business Development, it's because we're working on the symptoms of the problem, rather than the real problem. Getting to the root, or First Cause, of any real challenge, rather than just dealing with the symptoms, is what counts. This ability to delve deeper not only makes us successful in our roles, but also provides value to the prospect in helping to uncover their real issues.

As we challenge ourselves to improve, we tend to work diligently in constructing our process, refining our skills, establishing our goals and working our plans. These are all good left-brained, quantitative approaches. However we need to work on the right-brained side of the challenge too. This means learning to risk and to fail, maintaining a healthy self-concept, communicating our purpose early, establishing our long-term mission in life and continually measuring ourselves against our principles, values and ethics.

In order to uncover the real cause of any problem, you need to understand yourself in both short-term and long-term thinking. You must also possess the ability to be a left-brained, quantitative individual as well as a right-brained, qualitative individual. Business Development Professionals understand that their success is a combination of who they are as individuals, the application of their knowledge competency and what they do mechanically with that knowledge. The strongest driver of success in the role of Business Development is not the left-brained, short-term mechanical perspective. Rather, it is the right-brained perspective that takes into account both long-term mission and your short-term purpose in the role that ensures your success.

To be successful in the role of Business Development, work as hard as possible on the problem, and even harder on yourself.

#48

The Problem a Prospect Brings You Is Almost Never a Technical Problem.

By nature, technical professionals are driven to solve problems. So, it's not surprising that many Business Development Professionals focus their efforts on uncovering technical problems. Technical problems are, however, typically just intellectual concerns unless they are converted to more basic, first-person, personal pains. To be most effective, you must translate these technical problems into how they affect the business, how they affect the financials, and more critically, how they concern the individuals involved. Unless these second and third-degree situations are addressed in your discussions, the purely technical issues you've uncovered have limited value.

Business Development Professionals know and understand the technical solutions and capabilities their products and services provide from a technical solution perspective. Translating these technical features and benefits into first-person, personal pain as they relate to people, business and money problems as well as learning how to focus on those issues, is key to success in Business Development.

The 4 Cornerstones of Business Development are *Technical, Business, Money* and *People Knowledge*. But, knowledge alone is of limited value. It is the application of knowledge that is valuable. Our challenge as Business Development Professionals is to understand what problems we solve from the prospect's perspective and how those problems affect them in more than purely technical ways.

#49

If You Sense It or Feel It, Say It Tactfully.

During a conversation with a prospect, if you sense something is incorrect or feel you are being misled or denied information … trust your feelings. First, identify and understand what triggered those feelings. Then you must deal with them in a mature and appropriate manner. As a Business Development Professional, you must learn to skillfully, tactfully and professionally express your feelings. This will force the issues to the surface, and if done correctly, will cause you to gain credibility with the prospect. If you discount it or deny it, you may lose credibility, miss opportunities and eventually suffer afterburn.

Afterburn occurs when a past event continues to affect your behavior. When you realize that something did not make sense and you did not confront or challenge it in a professional way, there is a chance the real problem or pain will go undetected and unresolved.

Too many professionals mistakenly take the principle of removing all feeling from the Business Development role too literally. Professionals must first know themselves and take ownership of their feelings. By doing so, they are comfortable in challenging and confronting prospects in what they say or do in a manner that ultimately benefits both parties.

#50

The Problem the Prospect Brings You Is Never the Real Problem.

Business Development Professionals learn that people ultimately buy to avoid or overcome what they perceive to be a problem, dissatisfaction or disappointment. People buy to avoid a negative, not to pursue a positive.

The negative is often described as the prospect's pain. It is important to understand that the prospect does not initially tell you what their pain really is. Even prospects who admit they have problems will tend to discount, intellectualize or deflect the real issue. They have learned that if they give the intellectual or superficial symptoms of the problem, the typical salesperson is satisfied. It is the responsibility of the Business Development Professional to dig behind the intellectual information provided and ask, "What does that mean? Why is that? What is the core issue driving this problem?" Using questions to get beyond symptoms to the root cause of the pain is rather like a medical practitioner asking probing questions during a medical examination.

Business Development Professionals understand the Principle of the First Cause which says, "For a person to have a need to buy, they must have a problem or issue to avoid." Identifying how that issue or problem affects a person on an individual basis is referred to as first-person, personal pain, which is the real driving force motivating an individual to seek a solution.

Business Development Professionals understand that the problems prospects bring are almost never the real problems, but rather the intellectualization, symptoms or deflecting issues relating to the problem.

First-person, personal pain is the real driving force motivating an individual to seek a solution.

#51

Your Prospects Don't Care About You ... But They Love to Talk About Themselves.

Prospects and individuals in general are self-centered and really only care about themselves. Given the opportunity, they are happy to discuss every detail of their world, situation and challenges. Listening to you talk about how wonderful your company is and how great your products and services are, doesn't make their top ten list.

After gathering all of the information on your prospect's company, products, services, market and financials, your tendency is to lump this data with your product knowledge and spill it during the interview. You are better off asking questions about what you already know through your homework. Why? Because this position allows you to really understand the person and situation from their perspective. You're seen as a business professional who is sincerely interested in what is important and relevant to them.

When engaging a prospective client, do you tend to fly through the bonding and positioning steps? Why are you in such a hurry? Your time invested in listening and learning early in the process plays a significant role in building a long-term business relationship. The foundation of trust you construct early on by asking the easy questions benefits you later when you must ask the hard, painful questions.

Let your prospects talk about themselves and their world.
They'll love to tell you, if you just ask and listen.

#52
No One Will Ever Get Mad at You for Doing Something They Gave You Permission to Do.

We present this insight in *Wining Conversations: Mastering the Art of Business Development* and are always surprised by the number of individuals that remark, "Why didn't I think of that earlier?"

A Business Development Professional learns to be forthright

with their prospects and clients. Early in the relationship, they convey what they are aiming to accomplish, ask for permission and then follow through with their plan. What many of us fail to understand is that we are able to take the initiative in a business relationship. In fact, we can drive the agenda, but only if we get the other party's permission up front. This is the most basic of the Rules, Rights and Responsibilities. You simply ask permission for what you want to do! This must be conveyed in a professional, tactful and confident manner. Remember, you are asking for permission to ask questions, to be forthright, to discuss money, to understand the decision making process and to explore the real problems!

The first challenge of a Business Development Professional is to know what they aim to accomplish on the call, and then ask for permission to proceed. By seeking your client's permission to ask questions, it will be easier to follow your plan to a successful and prosperous relationship.

#53
The Burden of Proof Is on the Prospect.

Traditional sales people labor under an unfair burden and disadvantage. Psychologically, they believe that when approaching a potential customer, they have to prove the value of their product or service. Because of this misconception, they immediately begin promoting or pushing features and benefits, and consequently meet resistance from the prospect.

The MBD^i Business Development Process® is uniquely different. It's based on the understanding that without the prospect acknowledging they have a problem and wishing to solve it, there is no need to promote features and benefits. The key is getting the prospect to see, acknowledge and own their problems. The burden of proof is on the prospect initially acknowledging a problem, and then ultimately wanting a solution. In the final analysis, your challenge is to get the prospects to prove this to themselves. This shift in thinking and process takes all the pressure off the Business Development Professional. Through Socratic questioning, done in a nurturing way, the professional will be able to allow the prospect the opportunity to prove their position.

An insightful client once shared: "If the prospect can't prove to you that they have a problem, why are you trying to prove that you have a solution?"

#54

Why People Don't Buy: No Pain, No Match, No Crisis, No Trust.

Frequently in our Business Development process, we encounter prospects that decide not to buy. If we do not understand how and why people buy or have a process to disqualify unqualified opportunities early, we tend to rationalize a reason why the person did not buy from us. On a fundamental basis, there are four reasons why a person will not pursue a solution to a problem.

1. There is no problem; there is no pain. Therefore, there is no motivation, no call to action to pursue a solution.

2. There is no match. Specifically, the solution presented does not adequately address the problems uncovered.

3. There is no immediacy or urgency to solve the problem. The effect or impact of the situation is not critical enough to motivate your prospect to pursue the solution immediately.

4. There is no trust. This is the most important reason. You have not established the relationship wherein your prospect believes that your purpose—helping them figure out what they need or want and finding a solution, whether or not they purchase it from you—is truly ahead of your goal of making the sale.

Look back at all of the situations where your prospect or customer did not buy. You will find that one of these four, or a combination of these reasons, ultimately resulted in the final decision. An effective Business Development process requires that you know how and why people buy, engender your prospect's trust and respect, uncover their true issues, allow them to prioritize how to address these issues and provide adequate solutions.

#55

Your Prospect Needs to Be Working As Hard to Buy As You Are to Sell.

One of the basic rules of psychology states, "If you are working harder to help someone than they are working to help themselves, you are in fact the problem." When applying this to the Business Development role, it becomes apparent that too many traditional sales people are working much harder to sell something than the prospect is working to buy it.

In a balanced relationship, it is incumbent upon the prospect to acknowledge their problem and their desire to solve it both to themselves and to the Business Development Professional. The willingness to identify, quantify and detail the scope and depth of their problem is the responsibility of the prospect. It is the Business Development Professional's responsibility to ask insightful questions regarding the situation that solicits thought, reflective evaluation and motivation to act. A Business Development Professional comfortably and inquisitively engages the prospect in Socratic questioning, allowing the individual to discover and focus on the actual problem, acknowledge the scope of it and become motivated to solve it. The Business Development Professional simply facilitates the process wherein they allow the prospect to seek a solution to their problem, whether they provide it or not.

It is through this reflective dialogue that trust and understanding are established, the scope of the problem is understood by both parties and a partnership is established to seek the solution. The prospect is indeed working just as hard to get their problem solved as the Business Development Professional is to provide a solution.

#56
No Problem ... No Need
... No Prospect!

In Business Development, most of us think you have to establish a prospect's need for your product or service. But there's a significant hurdle that must be tackled first: the real problem. In order to have a need, there has to be something driving that need.

Psychology teaches that people are driven either to avoid pain or pursue pleasure. The strongest, most basic force is avoiding or overcoming a threat or pain. For a prospect to need a solution, this need must be propelled by the desire to avoid or overcome an existing problem. Most of us don't dig deep enough to find this out. We often look for a problem and take the symptom of that problem as its First Cause. We are unwilling to ask the probing questions necessary to uncover the First Cause that's motivating a prospect to pursue a solution.

This pain-developing expertise is based on the Socratic Method. Socrates believed that we grow through a continual questioning of the fundamental concepts of life: What is good? What is just?

What is right? He would claim ignorance and then lead his students through a participatory process of questioning the "what" and "why," resulting in understanding in a more full and fundamental manner. This questioning of all assumptions to get to the core truth is now called the Socratic Method. In order to get to the First Cause of your prospect's pain, you must use this technique, returning question for question until an understanding of the real problem is finally revealed. Only then is it appropriate to talk about possible solutions.

#57

Just Because You Have It ... Doesn't Mean They Need It!

Salespeople often rely too heavily on their company's products, services and accompanying solutions. They believe just because they have something to offer, someone must need it. Since that's not necessarily the case, they enter into business relationships with an unconscious liability.

People do not buy things based on need. Need is the pursuit of a positive. Buying is not based upon pursuing a positive, but involves overcoming or eliminating a negative. If there's no issue, problem or concern, there's no need for a solution.

Salespeople often assume either that everyone *should* or that everyone *does* need what they offer. They burden themselves with proving to prospects that needs do exist. That's a push relationship. Even if prospects do have problems to solve, most would deny it when pushed. Relationships like these are inherently flawed. There's a difference between trying to sell individuals on their needs versus helping them buy products or pursue solutions based on their perceptions of problems.

For validation, ask a client what concerns were eliminated or problems solved by purchasing your product or service, from their perspective. You cannot create a need where one does not exist. You cannot solve problems or eliminate pain where none are present. You can, however, become the problem by trying to convince people of needs that don't exist or concerns they don't have.

Beware of the trap: just because you have it ... doesn't mean they need it!

10

CHAPTER TEN:

Client Engagement Skill Insights

These three insights cover the client engagement skills necessary for success in the role of Business Development.

#58

If Your Question Is Longer Than Two Lines, You Probably Aren't Asking the Best Question.

Stop and take a moment to think about the kinds of questions you ask your prospects. Is your tendency to ask long, overly-focused questions or short, open-ended questions? As a Business Development Professional, it is critical to understand the value of a good question since it is the primary way to gather valuable Intel. However, it is important to note that not all questions are created equal. Over the years we have found that short, simple questions often elicit a more valuable and complete response. As you deliver your question to the prospect, be sure you are not "leading the witness" by asking long-winded questions or starting the question with a statement.

Scripting your questions prior to a call is invaluable in ensuring your questions are aimed at gathering the Intel you're looking for. Don't leave good questions to chance. The ability to instinctively think of relevant questions with appropriate follow-ons under pressure is not natural. Writing crystallizes thought. Take the time to put your thoughts and questions on paper. It will help you to remember your questions and respond under pressure.

Even as experienced as Larry King is, he always scripted his questions before his broadcast interviews. The advice he gave to up-and-coming presenters was to focus on the questions they asked to ensure they were always less than two lines. If they were longer than that, he suggested that they ask the question in a different way. When asked what his all-time favorite question was, he responded, "Why?"

One of the more powerful ways you can learn to ask good questions is to master the art of Socratic questioning. Socratic questioning seeks to get the other person to answer their own questions by making them think, and thereby drawing the answer out from them. This is a very valuable skill to learn.

Great storytellers have learned to never let the truth get in the way of a good story. Likewise, never let your questions hamper your ability to gather the human Intel, the HUMINT®, you need.

#59

Don't Get Mad At People For Doing What You Never Told Them Not to Do.

As professionals in Business Development we have to take responsibility for the nature of our relationship with our customer. Prevent issues from becoming negative issues by negotiating and agreeing on the rules of engagement at the beginning of the relationship. Create a win-win relationship and everybody succeeds.

Your prospects expect you to communicate your purpose, process and guidelines for doing business up front. Through discussion, discover right away if there are going to be difficulties in any aspect of doing business. Bring out the issues, discuss them and resolve them if possible. If an issue cannot be solved, you must have appropriate rules of engagement established to work around it. Establish your ability to manage a professional Business Development relationship by communicating the requirements and rules early on. This way, both sides can work in a positive and mutually beneficial manner, respecting the investment of each other's time, resources and desire to seek solutions to problems. Maintain control of your "reasoning adult" side and don't allow your "emotional child" to take control if something goes wrong because you failed to discuss it up front. Prospects and clients don't read minds any better than you or I do.

Communicate the rules of the relationship early, avoid misunderstandings and hold yourself fully accountable for the outcome of the relationship.

#60
You Will Never Listen Yourself Out of Business.

This insight is one of the better understood principles relating to the difference between traditional sales and Business Development. Simply put, if your objective is to develop business with your prospects, you learn more by asking questions and listening than by doing the talking.

Traditional salespeople have a need to educate prospects on their problems and the solutions which only they have to offer. They are convinced that this process will educate the prospects into buying their products or services. The fatal flaw in this thinking is assuming the prospect is ignorant. That's a lethal assumption. Prospects know what their world looks like, what problems they are experiencing and what motivates them to engage with someone in getting solutions. You win over your prospects by listening to them rather than telling and selling them.

Mastering Socratic questioning, asking intellectually and emotionally challenging questions and truly listening to the prospect is the mark of a true Business Development Professional. Your credibility is determined by the level and type of questions you ask, not the statements you make.

Win over your prospects by listening to them, not telling and selling them.

Additional Resources

About MBD*i*

Mastering Business Development, Inc. (MBD*i*) founded in 1979, is an international management consulting services firm. Our mission is to drive revenue growth through organizational change by providing Business Development resources, elevated thinking, knowledge, processes and skills while remaining committed to the core values of accountability, integrity, trust and mutual respect.

We provide solutions for your firm's revenue growth challenges by:

- Conducting present state Business Development assessments and formulating recommendations;
- Building, integrating or turning around Business Development organizations;
- Developing and implementing strategic, operational and tactical Business Development plans;
- Evaluating and sourcing Business Development leaders and personnel;
- Designing and implementing Business Development and business acquisition processes that guarantee revenue growth;
- Designing, developing and delivering standard, customized or tailored Business Development curricula.

We assist your organization to achieve revenue growth by:

- Driving strategic growth to ensure a full opportunity pipeline;
- Protecting your current revenue base while expanding organic growth;

- Implementing a proactive and client-centric Business Development culture;
- Leveraging existing personnel, client relationships and organizational resources to improve revenue results;
- Merging and integrating diverse business operations and new acquisitions.

MBD^i has provided Business Development services to the following industries for over thirty years. Our continued efforts are focused on providing the most effective revenue growth specific resources to complement this range of highly technical industries.

- Government services contractors
- Consulting engineering services
- Nuclear, power, energy and utility
- Economic development
- Information technology
- Biotechnology and pharmaceutical
- Consulting, business and professional services

Previous Publications

Winning Conversations: Mastering the Art of Business Development is the definitive manual for understanding how to develop business written by William B. Scheessele. This text explains the MBD^i proprietary and trademarked process and the 12 Core Competencies of Business Development, the benchmarks for professionals in revenue generating roles. Includes description of the 4 Cornerstones of Business Development and how to utilize them to achieve win/win situations for the individual, the company and the client.

Glossary

12 Core competencies of business development
The twelve basic leadership, knowledge and process competencies necessary to succeed in the role of Business Development.

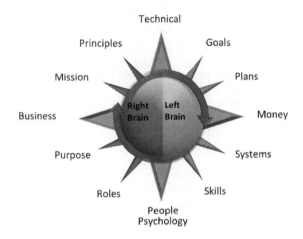

4 Cornerstones of business development
See *Technical Knowledge, Business Knowledge, Money Knowledge* and *People Knowledge*.

Adult ego state
Primarily analytical and quantitative, makes decisions based on logic and objective information. Reference *Games People Play: The Basic Handbook of Transactional Analysis* by Dr. Eric Berne.

Afterburn
When a preceding event continues to have a psychological effect on one's present behavior.

Alpha-wolf
Dominant leader personality profile.

Blue bird opportunity
An opportunity that comes out of nowhere and closes unexpectedly.

Business acquisition process
Government terminology for Business Development process of end-to-end revenue generation.

Business culture
See *culture*.

Business knowledge
Knowledge of one's own business, but more importantly, knowledge of the prospect's business resulting in an understanding of the effects of the solutions one provides to the prospect. One of the 4 *Cornerstones of Business Development*.

Child ego state
Makes decisions based on emotion. Three divisions of the Child Ego State are adaptive, rebellious and natural. Ego state that decides whether one feels OK or Not OK. Reference *Games People Play: The Basic Handbook of Transactional Analysis* by Dr. Eric Berne. See *OK*.

Client engagement process
A multi-phase, multi-step process to gather high value human Intel (see *HUMINT®*) as part of an *Opportunity Identification and Qualification Phase*.

Conceptual limitations
Psychological challenges that may impede one's performance in the Business Development role.

Culture
The sum of the principles, values, ethics and level of thinking of the individuals within an organization.

Disqualify opportunities
See *Opportunity Identification and Qualification*.

Emotional child
See *Child Ego State*.

Farmers
Personnel predominantly focused on expanding existing contracts or accounts.

Goal
The end toward which effort is directed.

Goal-driven culture
Business Development thinking and behavior that is short-term, revenue based and founded on internal need.

Government acquisition policies
Purchasing policies followed by the government when procuring products or services.

HUMINT®
High value human Intel.

Hunters
Personnel predominantly focused on developing new opportunities for an organization.

Intel gathering
The ability, skills and experience to gather intelligence to support decision making.

Intrepreneurial
Describes the thinking and behavior of an intrepreneur. The intrepreneur takes on the responsibility to run an area or part of an organization like their own enterprise and embraces the responsibility to reach revenue and profit objectives in true partnership with their employer.

Left-brained
Left-brained thinking is objective thinking that focuses on the quantitative, logical, measurable and predictive part of our personalities.

Long-term opportunity
See *strategic opportunity*.

Money knowledge
Knowledge of how clients make money and how helping clients get their problems solved enhances the financial benefit to the client. One of the 4 *Cornerstones of Business Development*.

(OI&Q)^i phase
See *Opportunity Identification and Qualification*.

OK
OK feelings come from being assured and confident in various situations. See *Child Ego State*.

Operational and tactical plans
Business Development planning and execution specific to goals, plans, systems and skills for developing short to midterm opportunities.

Opportunity identification and qualification phase
The early identification and qualification or disqualification of revenue opportunities. (OI&Q)^i is a priority term specific to gathering high value human Intel to enhance the value of this phase of a Business Development process.

Organizational culture
See *culture*.

Pain
Negative emotional tension. What drives people to purchase.

Peddler mentality
See *traditional sales*.

People knowledge
Knowledge of behavioral psychology, understanding what drives one's own behavior as well as the behavior of prospects and clients. One of the 4 *Cornerstones of Business Development*.

Personality driven
Business Development engagement process based on the personality of the individual executing it.

Principle of the first cause
In Business Development, the theory that the foundational pain which is often disguised or hidden requires one to continually question through the initial described symptoms to dig down to the real problem.

Proactive
Acting in anticipation of future problems, needs, or changes. In Business Development, refers to direct Client Engagement early in the buying process.

Prospect
An individual that has an issue or pain for which one has a potential solution.

Purpose
In Business Development, one's purpose is to help clients meet their needs whether or not they purchase a solution from you.

Purpose-driven culture
Long-term, client-focused, service-based thinking and Business Development behavior.

Purpose statement
Used to communicate your purpose in an engagement to a prospect or client.

Push-sell
See *traditional sales*.

Qualification
See *Opportunity Identification and Qualification Phase*.

Reactive
Tending to be responsive or to react to a stimulus. In Business Development, refers to late involvement in the buying process, usually just responding to *Requests for Proposals* or Requests for Information.

Reasoning adult
See *Adult Ego State*.

Request for proposal
A solicitation for firm offers which become binding contracts upon acceptance; can contain multiple evaluation factors and require multivolume response.

Return on investment
Profits in relation to capital invested.

RFP
See *Request for Proposal*.

Right-brained
Right-brained thinking is intuitive, creative, log-term, strategic, abstract and philosophical.

ROI
See *return on investment*.

Role-identity
What we do in our various life roles.

Rules, rights and responsibilities
Establishing the rights of each party in the relationship.

Self-identity
Who we are as individuals.

Shaping
Shaping occurs when you *ethically* influence customer requirements or decision making to improve your probability of winning.

Short-term opportunity
A revenue opportunity likely to materialize and award within an annual revenue period.

Socrates
Classical Greek Athenian philosopher credited as one of the founders of Western philosophy.

Socratic method (questioning)
Disciplined questioning used to explore complex ideas, to get to the truth of things, to open up issues and problems or to control the discussion.

Source selection committee
A group of decision makers utilized in the US government acquisition process to select the winner of a bid contest.

Strategic opportunity
An opportunity expected to have a significant long-term financial impact or a significant impact on the growth of the company's business.

Technical knowledge
Knowledge of the technical aspects of a prospect's or client's problem and the potential solution. One of the *4 Cornerstones of Business Development*.

Traditional sales
Sales philosophy that emphasizes features and benefits, is quota-driven, narrow in focus and based on the seller's solution versus the buyer's pain.

Turning around
Reversing the decline of a company or firm by restructuring and refocusing the Business Development organization.

Alphabetical List of Insights

Made in the USA
Middletown, DE
11 July 2021